GW01607586
Please write your nam
ou filled out.
Page 2-5
Page 6-9
Page 10-13
Page 14-17
Page 18-21
Page 22-25
Page 26-29
Page 30-33
Page 34-37
Page 38-41
Page 42-45
Page 46-49
Page 50-53
Page 54-57
Page 58-61

This log belongs to:

Copyright © Kids Adventure Logs Ltd 2023

www.kidsadventurelogs.com

Instructions Page
(read me!)

Welcome to my friends' log!

Please choose a blank spread and answer as many questions as you like!

On the following spread, please write something about yourself and stick some cool pictures of you, your pets, your family, (anything!). You can also ask ME a question there!

Thank you for taking part! I will treasure this log for the years to come!

shine on
Venus
Mercury
Name:
Do you have a nickname?
Earth
Mars
When is your birthday?
What is your zodiac sign?
Uranus
What's your favourite thing to do?
Jupiter
Who is your favourite artist or singer?
Saturn
What's your favourite song?
What's your favourite holiday?
Neptune
What's your first childhood memory?
A

Do you have a pet?

What is it?

What is their name?

Who is your crush?

(You do **NOT** have to answer this.)

What's your favourite animal?

What's your favourite colour?

What's your favourite book?

Do you want to ask me any questions?

What do you want to know about me?

about me

Write something you want me to know about you or draw/stick a picture of something you like!

You can also stick in a photo of yourself and/or draw something!

shine on
Venus
Mercury
Name:
Do you have a nickname?
When is your birthday?
Earth
Mars
What is your zodiac sign?
Uranus
What's your favourite thing to do?
Jupiter
Who is your favourite artist or singer?
What's your favourite song?
Saturn
What's your favourite holiday?
Neptune
What's your first childhood memory?
A

Do you have a pet?

What is it?

What is their name?

Who is your crush?

(You do **NOT** have to answer this.)

What's your favourite animal?

What's your favourite colour?

What's your favourite book?

Do you want to ask me any questions?

What do you want to know about me?

about me
Write something you want me to know about you or draw/stick a picture of something you like!

You can also stick in a photo of yourself and/or draw something!

shine on
Venus
Mercury
Name:
Do you have a nickname?
Earth
Mars
When is your birthday?
What is your zodiac sign?
Uranus
What's your favourite thing to do?
Jupiter
Who is your favourite artist or singer?
Saturn
What's your favourite song?
What's your favourite holiday?
Neptune
What's your first childhood memory?
A

Do you have a pet?

What is it?

What is their name?

Who is your crush?

(You do **NOT** have to answer this.)

What's your favourite animal?

What's your favourite colour?

What's your favourite book?

Do you want to ask me any questions?

What do you want to know about me?

about me

Write something you want me to know about you or draw/stick a picture of something you like!

You can also stick in a photo of yourself and/or draw something!

shine on
Venus
Mercury
Name:
Do you have a nickname?
Earth
Mars
When is your birthday?
What is your zodiac sign?
Uranus
What's your favourite thing to do?
Jupiter
Who is your favourite artist or singer?
Saturn
What's your favourite song?
What's your favourite holiday?
Neptune
What's your first childhood memory?
A

Do you have a pet?

What is it?

What is their name?

Who is your crush?

(You do **NOT** have to answer this.)

What's your favourite animal?

What's your favourite colour?

What's your favourite book?

Do you want to ask me any questions?

What do you want to know about me?

about me
Write something you want me to know about you or draw/stick a picture of something you like!

You can also stick in a photo of yourself and/or draw something!

shine on
Venus
Mercury
Name:
Do you have a nickname?
Earth
Mars
When is your birthday?
What is your zodiac sign?
Uranus
What's your favourite thing to do?
Jupiter
Who is your favourite artist or singer?
What's your favourite song?
Saturn
What's your favourite holiday?
Neptune
What's your first childhood memory?
A

Do you have a pet?
What is it?
What is their name?
Who is your crush?
(You do NOT have to answer this.)
What's your favourite animal?
What's your favourite colour?
What's your favourite book?
Journal
Do you want to ask me any questions?
What do you want to know about me?

Write something you want me to know about you or draw/stick a picture of something you like!

You can also stick in a photo of yourself and/or draw something!

Name:

Do you have a nickname?

When is your birthday?

What is your zodiac sign?

What's your favourite thing to do?

Who is your favourite artist or singer?

What's your favourite song?

What's your favourite holiday?

What's your first childhood memory?

Do you have a pet?

What is it?

What is their name?

Who is your crush?

(You do NOT have to answer this.)

What's your favourite animal?

What's your favourite colour?

What's your favourite book?

Do you want to ask me any questions?

What do you want to know about me?

about me
Write something you want me to know about you or draw/stick a picture of something you like!

You can also stick in a photo of yourself and/or draw something!

shine on
Venus
Mercury
Name:
Do you have a nickname?
Earth
Mars
When is your birthday?
What is your zodiac sign?
Uranus
What's your favourite thing to do?
Jupiter
Who is your favourite artist or singer?
Saturn
What's your favourite song?
What's your favourite holiday?
Neptune
What's your first childhood memory?
A

Do you have a pet?

What is it?

What is their name?

Who is your crush?

(You do NOT have to answer this.)

What's your favourite animal?

What's your favourite colour?

What's your favourite book?

Do you want to ask me any questions?

What do you want to know about me?

about me
Write something you want me to know about you or draw/stick a picture of something you like!

You can also stick in a photo of yourself and/or draw something!

shine on
Venus
Mercury
Name:
Do you have a nickname?
Earth
Mars
When is your birthday?
What is your zodiac sign?
Uranus
Jupiter
What's your favourite thing to do?
Who is your favourite artist or singer?
Saturn
What's your favourite song?
What's your favourite holiday?
Neptune
What's your first childhood memory?
A

Do you have a pet?

What is it?

What is their name?

Who is your crush?
(You do NOT have to answer this.)

What's your favourite animal?

What's your favourite colour?

What's your favourite book?

Do you want to ask me any questions?
What do you want to know about me?

about me
Write something you want me to know about you or draw/stick a picture of something you like!

You can also stick in a photo of yourself and/or draw something!

shine on
Venus
Mercury
Name:
Do you have a nickname?
Earth
Mars
When is your birthday?
What is your zodiac sign?
Uranus
Jupiter
What's your favourite thing to do?
Who is your favourite artist or singer?
Saturn
What's your favourite song?
What's your favourite holiday?
Neptune
What's your first childhood memory?
A

Do you have a pet?

What is it?

What is their name?

Who is your crush?

(You do **NOT** have to answer this.)

What's your favourite animal?

What's your favourite colour?

What's your favourite book?

Do you want to ask me any questions?

What do you want to know about me?

about me
Write something you want me to know about you or draw/stick a picture of something you like!

You can also stick in a photo of yourself and/or draw something!

shine on
Venus
Mercury
Name:
Do you have a nickname?
When is your birthday?
Earth
Mars
What is your zodiac sign?
Uranus
What's your favourite thing to do?
Jupiter
Who is your favourite artist or singer?
Saturn
What's your favourite song?
What's your favourite holiday?
Neptune
What's your first childhood memory?
A

Do you have a pet?

What is it?

What is their name?

Who is your crush?

(You do **NOT** have to answer this.)

What's your favourite animal?

What's your favourite colour?

What's your favourite book?

Do you want to ask me any questions?

What do you want to know about me?

about me
Write something you want me to know about you or draw/stick a picture of something you like!

You can also stick in a photo of yourself and/or draw something!

shine on
Venus
Mercury
Name:
Do you have a nickname?
Earth
Mars
When is your birthday?
What is your zodiac sign?
Uranus
Jupiter
What's your favourite thing to do?
Who is your favourite artist or singer?
Saturn
What's your favourite song?
What's your favourite holiday?
Neptune
What's your first childhood memory?
A

Do you have a pet?

What is it?

What is their name?

Who is your crush?

(You do **NOT** have to answer this.)

What's your favourite animal?

What's your favourite colour?

What's your favourite book?

Do you want to ask me any questions?

What do you want to know about me?

Write something you want me to know about you or draw/stick a picture of something you like!

You can also stick in a photo of yourself and/or draw something!

shine on
Venus
Mercury
Name:
Do you have a nickname?
Earth
Mars
When is your birthday?
What is your zodiac sign?
Uranus
What's your favourite thing to do?
Jupiter
Who is your favourite artist or singer?
Saturn
What's your favourite song?
What's your favourite holiday?
Neptune
What's your first childhood memory?
A

Do you have a pet?

What is it?

What is their name?

Who is your crush?

(You do **NOT** have to answer this.)

What's your favourite animal?

What's your favourite colour?

What's your favourite book?

Do you want to ask me any questions?

What do you want to know about me?

Write something you want me to know about you or draw/stick a picture of something you like!

You can also stick in a photo of yourself and/or draw something!

shine on
Venus
Mercury
Name:
Do you have a nickname?
When is your birthday?
Earth
Mars
What is your zodiac sign?
Uranus
What's your favourite thing to do?
Jupiter
Who is your favourite artist or singer?
What's your favourite song?
Saturn
What's your favourite holiday?
Neptune
What's your first childhood memory?
A

Do you have a pet?

What is it?

What is their name?

Who is your crush?

(You do **NOT** have to answer this.)

What's your favourite animal?

What's your favourite colour?

What's your favourite book?

Do you want to ask me any questions?

What do you want to know about me?

about me
Write something you want me to know about you or draw/stick a picture of something you like!

You can also stick in a photo of yourself and/or draw something!

shine on
Venus
Mercury
Name:
Do you have a nickname?
Earth
Mars
When is your birthday?
What is your zodiac sign?
Uranus
What's your favourite thing to do?
Jupiter
Who is your favourite artist or singer?
What's your favourite song?
Saturn
What's your favourite holiday?
Neptune
What's your first childhood memory?
A

Do you have a pet?

What is it?

What is their name?

Who is your crush?

(You do NOT have to answer this.)

What's your favourite animal?

What's your favourite colour?

What's your favourite book?

Do you want to ask me any questions?

What do you want to know about me?

about me
Write something you want me to know about you or draw/stick a picture of something you like!

You can also stick in a photo of yourself and/or draw something!

Name:

Do you have a nickname?

When is your birthday?

What is your zodiac sign?

What's your favourite thing to do?

Who is your favourite artist or singer?

What's your favourite song?

What's your favourite holiday?

What's your first childhood memory?

Do you have a pet?

What is it?

What is their name?

Who is your crush?

(You do NOT have to answer this.)

What's your favourite animal?

What's your favourite colour?

What's your favourite book?

Do you want to ask me any questions?

What do you want to know about me?

about me
Write something you want me to know about you or draw/stick a picture of something you like!

You can also stick in a photo of yourself and/or draw something!

Printed in Great Britain
by Amazon